ANCIENT OLYMPIA

THEODORA G. KARAGHIORGA
Keeper of Antiquities

EDITIONS APOLLO

The following guides have been published by the APOLLON Publishers and can be obtained at the corresponding archaeological sites:

	By the Archaeologists
Athens Byzantine Museum	Manolis Chatzidakis
Minoan Civilisation and Knossos Palace	Sonia di Neuhoff
The Acropolis and its Museum	M. Brouscaris
The Acropolis	M. Brouscaris
Copper Items of the Athens National Archaeological Museum	Basil G. Callipolitis
Delphi	Efie Touloupa
Ancient Olympia	Sonia di Neuhoff
Ancient Corinth	Dora Karageorga
Marble Masterpieces of the Athens Archaeological Museum	Sonia di Neuhoff
	Dimitrios Papastamou

To be published

Vases of the Athens National Archaeological Museum	Barbara Philippaki
Mycenaean Collection of the Athens National Archaeological Museum	John Sakkelarakis
Cycladic Collection of the Athens National Archaeological Museum	Efie Sapouna-Sakkelaraki
Lindos	Sonia di Neuhoff
Mycenae-Mycenaean Art	
Corfou	
Epidaurus	

Cover Illustrations: *front*: Zeus and Ganymede terracotta group 470 b.C.
rear: Eastern colonnade of the Palestra.
Translated by: Fifi P. Velendza.
Photographies: «Hannibal».
© E. Tzaferis, S.A., 52, rue Phokionos Négri - Athenes, 1971.
Printed by H. Fournier, S.A. - Vitoria - Spain.

ANCIENT OLYMPIA

Some 15 kms. from the mouth of Alfios river on the Ionian Sea, on its right bank, at the very spot where it meets the Kladeos river coming from the north, flourished the most famous panhellenic religious and cultural center of the ancient world, the Sanctuary of Olympia. This sweet and quiet site where the peaceful waters of Alfios wind through green hills, where the air is warm and iridescent, with open skies around the valley, has become a natural frame for the principles of peace and national unity of the hellenes, principles which were glorified through the 1000-year history of Olympia.

1. History of Olympia.

a) *Founding of the Sanctuary - The First Games.*

The archaeological findings in the area ascertain the fact that it was inhabited since 2,500 b.C. Early Greek vases were discovered in the northern dike of the Stadium and arched constructions of the early 2nd millenium b.C. were uncovered by the temple of Hera, the Metroon and the Pelopion.

The cemeteries found in the area of the modern Museum, and the slopes of the hill standing Northwest of the Kronion mountain prove the existence of worthwhile mycenean settlements. There can be little doubt that these were connected to Pisa and its early achaean inhabitants, who, tradition says, were the first masters of the sanctuary. The mythology of the area brought into later times traces of prehistoric mycenean life. These stories were mostly relating of the sanctuary and its games, especially the charriot contest between Oenomaos, king of Pisa and Pelops the grandfather of Agamemnon, king of Mycenae.

As in Delphi, Gaia was worshipped in Olympia with her oracle standing at the foot of Kronion Mountain. Rea, or Mother of Gods, was worshipped at Ideon Andron, also near the Kronion. Yet nothing was left of these two ancient sanctuaries. The first concrete indications of the existence of a holy place in the locality of the sanctuary do not come before the 12th century b.C. An empty grave was found under the tomb of Pelops (Pelopion) dating to appr. 1100 b.C. while the earliest offerings to the sanctuary go back to the 11th and the 10th centuries b.C. They are mostly earthenware and bronze statuettes portraying human beings, horses, bulls, «synoris» two-horse charriots, and bronze tripods. The latter categories are more related to the legend and the worship of Pelops, consequently leading to the conclusion that ever since the early Geometric Era chariot contests were organised in his memory with bronze tripods, which Homer names «Athla», as prizes to the winners. It is not certain whether the first sponsors of these races were the former inhabitants of the area, the Pisates or the dorian settlers of Elis who, led by their king Oxylon, conquered North-western Peloponesus in the 12th century b.C. At any rate the Elians seem to have had full control over the sanctuary in the 8th century.

In 776 b.C. king Ifitos of Elis reorganised the games, replacing the charriot races by foot running contests of one «stadion» (192.27 m.). The first winner was Koryvos from Elis. The Olympic games were set to be held at intervals of five years and 776 b.C., birth-year of the games, was fixed as the first year of the Olympiad calendar, which, though used by many ancient writers, did not meet with acceptance by all the then hellenic world.

And with the creation of new legends on the origins of the Games the sovereignty of the Elians over Olympia is established with Zeus, the father-god of the Dorians, as the protecting deity of the sanctuary. The games, which were formerly held in memory of Pelops, were now made in Zeus' honour while Hercules, his son and protector of king Oxylos of the Elians, was their alleged founder. All legends not related to the Elians were rejected. Hercules from Thebes was supposed to have set the length of the Stadium of Olympia at 600 ft, to have traced the sides of the «Altis», Zeus' sacred wood, the transplanting of the olive tree by the Northerners, etc.

Ifitos, anxious to attain full success of the games, signed a peace truce with Sparta and Pisa, thereby making it possible for athletes and sports fans from the whole country to reach Olympia through lands usually at war. This truce became the origin of the panhelle-nic sacred truce, which at first lasted one and later three months during which all belligerency stopped; no death sentence was exe-cuted nor were any differences discussed. Fear of never again being admitted in the sanctuary and of Zeus' punishment preserved ge-neral peace and established Olympia's position as guardian of national unity of the Greeks. It appears from the lists of game win-ners that at first most athletes came from Elis, Achaia and Messinia. In the 7th century they came mostly from Sparta; later more of them came from the Greek towns of S. Italy and Sicily thus having all Greece participating in the games but still with a majority of Dorians, which prevailed all through the long history of the Games.

No buildings or temples existed in the area until the end of the Geometric Era. Wild olive-trees and poplars embraced the tomb of Pelops, the altar of Zeus —which was gradually growing from the accumulated cindres of sacrificed animals— the altars of Hes-tia and several other deities. Numerous votive offerings, such as tripods, idols and weapons were standing around the altars or hanging from the trees of the temple. At first foot races were made over one stadion and used to take place within the Altis with Pe-lops' tomb as the finishing line, later moved to the altar of Zeus. In 724 b.C. «diavlos» was added (double stadion distance) and in 720 b.C. the «dolihos» (24 stadia). By the end of the 8th century the games had been enriched with the «pentathlon» and wrestling.

b) *Days of Glory.*
1) Archaic Era (7th-6th century b.C.).

During this time the sanctuary lived through days of fast de-velopment and growing fame, with increased numbers of visitors and votive offerings. New style sports are added, reaching in 200 b.C. a total of eighteen.

Between 668 and 572 b.C. the Games were administered by the Pisates. The oldest building in the Altis was built then, around mid-7th century; it is the temple of Hera where the first statue of Zeus was placed. The temple was reconstructed much larger and elaborated in the 6th century, at which time the Bouleuterion and the Prytaneum of the Elians were erected. Yet the central worshipping

5

spot was still the altar of Zeus and the Pelopion to which a hexagonal enclosure was provided. The constantly growing number of visitors to the games brought about the creation of the first stadium in 550 b.C. Day after day the Stadium dikes fill with more and more statues of gods, heroes and game-winners, which, being so delicate and valuable, the cities decided to build a «treasury» each, at the foot of the Kronion, to preserve them.

2) Classical Era (5th-4th century b.C.).

The erection of the Temple of Zeus marks the peak in the life of the sanctuary and the games. The funds for the building of the temple came from the booty the Elians collected after their victory over the pro-dorian community of Pisa and Trifylia, who had revolted against them. Thus the Elians secured full control over Olympia and they reorganised and afforded glamour to the games and splendour to the area of the sanctuary.

Soon after the founding of the Temple (456 b.C.) the first Stadium (11) was built east of the archaic one but still within the Altis and still close to the altar of Zeus. The space outside the Altis was used as training area and for bathing installations.

The 4th century is characterised by intensive building, resulting in drastic changes in the form of the Altis. The temple of the Mother of Gods which is the smallest of the three temples was built during this period, then following the battle at Chaeronia the circular Philippeion, the most recent building in the Altis. On the whole the area is acquiring the characteristics of the trends of the art in those times which was tending to form rectangular constructions. Consequently the Altis was surrounded by galleries and yards. The landmarks of the western and southern sides were spotted by enclosures while the treasuries lined along the northern side of the Altis stood for northern boundaries. The Stadium underwent considerable changes by its transfer some 80 metres eastwards and its complete separation from the worship areas through the erection of the Echo Portico whose colonnade, together with that of the Northeastern Edifice, set a fixed eastern boundary for the sanctuary.

The South Portico constituted a monumental façade overlooking Alfios River. Later, close to the end of the century, Leonidas from Naxos subsidized the erection of a vast hostel on the South-west, while the clergy was lodged in the Theokoleon. The Stadium on the other hand was rearranged so as to receive 40,000 persons.

These gorgeous new buildings together with the richness of the offerings, the glamour of the Games and the various other manifestations held parallel to the Games, made of Olympia a panhellenic cultural and political centre.

Famous artists like Onatas, Pythagoras, Myron, Polyklitos, Phidias, Praxitelis, Lysippos, Silanion, made splendid sculptures offered to and decorating the sacred buildings and the Altis in general. Olympia was visited by Anaxagoras, Plato, Aristoteles and other philosophers and tradition says that Thales and Chilon died here during the Games. Sophists like Prodikos, Gorgias and Ippias and orators as famous as Lysias and Isocrates delivered speeches with messages of panhellenic unity. Poets came here to immortalize game-winners in their verses. And Herodotus earned his fame reading out part of his «History» to the spectators from the rear end of the Temple of Zeus.

Yet this same period of glistening magnificence was breeding the first signs of degeneration, with the change in the nature of the Games, which had been, in their early stage, part of the worship dedicated to the god (who was «attending» them). In fact the crowning of a winner with a laurel wreath symbolised his secret merging with the god. The separation of the Stadium from the Altis could be taken as reflecting the abolition of the religious aspect of the Games, a parting with the sacred. As a result, however, the Games lost their significance in the spiritual and political life of the nation. Sports became professional, witnessing a few cases of corruption of athletes and judges; for it could not be a mere coincidence that for the first time the «Zannes» (statues of Zeus) appeared in the area —and these were usually made from fines inflicted upon bribed athletes. Such political manifestations as Themistocles' «triumph» in the Stadium, the destruction of the sumptuous stage of tyrant Dionysos as a result of the excitement that overtook the spectators from Lycias' speech in 388 b.C., the announcement of Alexander the Great's decree on the return of political refugees and the erection of the Philippeion by the Macedonias were not related to the worship of Zeus nor to panhellenic unity. The violation of the truce within the Altis is one more symptom of downfall. In fact the 420 b.C. games were held under armed protection for fear of an invasion by the Spartans. In 364 b.C. an actual battle took place between Elians, Arcadians and Pisates, when the latter two, who had undertaken the organisation of the games for that year, were pulled out by the Elians by force. Again in 312 b.C. Telesforos, a general in the army of Antigonus, invaded Olympia and marauded the temple's treasury. A hundred years later Philip the 5th settled for a while in the Leonideon. In spite of all these discouraging events Olympia remained for many centuries the primal link between the otherwise divided Greece, thanks to the deep tradition built around it.

c.) *Decline and Fall* (Hellenistic & Roman Eras).

As the Games were gradually turning into showy sports manifestations, the centre of interest shifted to the athletic areas outside the Altis. The Palestra and the Gymnasium were built from the 3rd to the 1st centuries b.C. for the training and lodging of athletes. The baths nearby were enlarged and improved and a monumental vaulted entrance («Krypti») for the athletes and a permanent platform were built for the jury and other officials. The festivities were constantly losing their religious aspect and Olympia was gradually turning into a place of presumptuous show-off of wealth and power for rulers of the hellenistic era (vide Ptolemee's votive offering).

The political weakening of the country and its defeat by the Romans affected the sanctuary even more. Mommius, the Roman general (146 b.C.) chose to hang on the pediments of the temple of Zeus shields of the Achaeans as trophies of his victory over them. Syllas on the other hand emptied the treasuries and confiscated several pieces of art. Six years later, in 80 b.C., he ordered the Games to be held in Rome as manifestations of his victory over Mithridates. Nero's passage is marked by the «immigration» of more pieces of art to Rome while the Games were replaced in 66 A.D. by a music contest of which he was the winner. Purely political expediency forced the Elians to invent mythological proofs which

8

would not show the Romans as barbarians thus permitting their participation in the Games. Tiberius Germanicus as well as Nero won first prizes in charriot races.

It is, however, thanks to the pax romana and the interest of Roman emperors that Olympia regained its oecumenical nature and the sanctuary as well as the Games witnessed an age of revival. As a token of gratitude the Elians introduced the worship of Augustus and they placed his statue in the Metroon, which was turned into a temple in his honour. The Games flourished anew under Hadrian. Part of the last improvement of the Stadium was the addition on its northern bank of new rows of seats. Herod Atticus later on subsidized the building of an aqueduct for the needs of the sanctuary and he had a monumental reservoir (the Exhedra) built and named after his wife Regilla. Almost all the existing buildings in the area were given a fresh touch; the Leonideon, the Bouleuterion, the Prytaneum, the Theokoleon, the Gymansium, the Palestra. Luxurious baths were erected in the northern, southern and western sides of the Altis, a new enclosure with majestic gates surrounds the Altis and Nero built a magnificent villa in the locality of the Northeastern Edifice.

The end of the age-old history of the temple begins with the invasion of the Herulians in 267 A.D. In an effort to rescue the most precious parts of the sanctuary, that is the Temple and the statue of Zeus, the sanctuary authorities destroyed parts of the Echo Portico, the Metroon, the Treasuries and the Leonideon and used their material to build a wall, 3.50 metres thick and 4 metres high, around the Temple and the Bouleuterion. This marks the end of the Olympic winners' lists of names custom, but the games continued to be held with the participation of numerous «barbarians».

The 291st Olympiad of the year 393 A.D. during the reign of Theodosius I was the last one; two years later Zeus' statue was taken to Constantinople only to be destroyed sometime later in a conflagration. By order of Theodosius II to destroy all pagan temples the Temple at Olympia was burnt down in 426 A.D. Two strong earthquakes in 522 and 551 A.D. completed the catastrophe. Beginning with the 5th century a small christian community settled in the area and it built a church over the place where Phidias workshop stood in the past. The church was built with whatever material was left from the ancient buildings. A slav settlement followed, leaving behind a cemetery close to the Museum. In the Middle Ages the inundations of Kladeos and Alfios rivers carried away lots of the ancient relics and the mud that was left behind covered the rest. The name of Olympia was forgotten; people called the area, up until the days excavations began, Serviana or Antilalos.

2. The Games.

The festivities and the games were performed up until the 2nd century A.D. in the same manner they had been organised in 472 b.C. with minor alterations.

Every free Greek had the right to participate; those excluded were non-Greeks, slaves, criminals, sacrilegists and, for purely religious reasons, married women —who were sentenced to death when violating this rule. Only the priestess of Demeter Chamyni could attend the games. Women would then organise, every four years, the Herea in honour of Hera with foot races of young girls in the Stadium.

Order and the organisation of the Games were assigned to Elian judges, at first two young men for each Olympiad who gradually reached a number of twelve. One month (according to some, 10 months) before the Games they would supervise the training of athletes in Elis and in Olympia. As time for the opening of the festivities came close heralds would leave from Olympia to declare the beginning of the sacred truce all over the country for the whole duration of the Games, including the days from their departure and up until their return. When the Games were at their best, thousands of visitors used to come, camp in the open and, according to writings of those days, they suffered heavy inconveniences due to the lack of water and especially from the heat. The festivities lasted five days and they usually took place on full-moon of the 8th month of the solar year, i.e. around the month of August.

The programme of the first day included listing of the names of the athletes and setting their position in the games each one would participate in, taking the oath by the judges before the altar of Zeus, in the Bouleuterion, the contest of trumpeters and heralds who would announce the names of the winners and finally the contests between children.

On the second day took place the games which survived since the days of the festivities commemorating Pelops, i.e. horseback races and charriot racing in the Hippodrome south of the Stadium. Best of all were the quadriga races, a rulers' game, where the owner of the horses and not the charrioteer was proclaimed as winner. This is how Kyniska, daughter of the Spartan king Archidamos, became an Olympiad winner. All charriots —at one time they had reached forty— had to go around the Hippodrome twelve times which made approximately fourteen kilometres.

The pentathlon would then follow in the Stadium (five games: foot racing, wrestling, javelin, discus, jumps) and in the evening as the sun went down and full moon would rise, funeral offerings were made at the Pelopion by the sacrifice of a «black ram».

The next day —third in line— the Elians sacrificed one hundred bulls on the altar of Zeus. The procession started at the Prytaneum, went along the outside part of the western yard, entered the Altis from the northwestern entrance and, walking along first the southern and then the eastern wall of the temple, ended up before the altar. More sacrifices were made on the various other altars in the Altis. The afternoon was devoted to various kinds of foot racing, i.e. stadion, dolihos, diavlos. The stadion racing (197.27 metres) and diavlos (2 × 197.27 metres) took place between four persons each time and the winners of each set would compete for the finals, the winner of which would ultimately be the «stadion winner» for the Olympiad. For dolihos on the other hand (24 × 192.57 metres) all runners would compete together.

The fourth day was covered by heavier sports like wrestling, boxing, "pagration" and racing with armories. "Pagration" was the wildest of all, a combination of wrestling and boxing with full freedom of strokes.

The last day would be devoted to awarding the prizes to the winners. Right after the end of each game the respective winner was provisionally crowned with ribbons and handed a palm leaf in his right hand. On this last day they would all parade before the cheering spectators, heading towards the temple of Zeus where they were crowned by the chief judge with the «cotinos», a branch from the olive-tree standing on the northwestern side of the temple. Sacrifices would follow on the altars, processions of the representatives of cities carrying their precious offerings, dinner for the winners at the Prytaneum. The whole night following, all the visitors to Olympia were fed either on the sacrifice meat or at the expense of wealthy winners (Alkibiades fed thousands of spectators in 416 b.C. to celebrate his three victories in quadriga racing). The whole area was filled with the sounds of hymns and triumphal songs of former Olympiad-winners. Such a scene is beautifully described by Pindarus in one of his poems on Olympia.

εν δ εσπερον
εφλεξεν ευωπιδος
σελανας ερατον φαος
αειδετο δε παν τεμενος
τερπναισι θαλιαις
τον εγκωμιον αμφι εροπον.

3. The Buildings of the Sanctuary.

(Figures in parentheses refer to designs on pages 21, 22).

Prytaneum (1, 2).

What is left of it is part of the roman remodelling which had very little of the original building of the 6th century b.C. The square room inside must have had the altar in the middle, where the fire of the public Hearth of the Elians burned. The large north peristylion and the rooms on the western side constituted the dining and cooking areas. During excavations the foundations of the Hestia altar, dating back to the geometric era, were uncovered (2).

Philippeion (3).

This is a rotunda of 12.24 metres diameter, built after the battle of Chaeronea by Philip II. 18 ionic columns supported a conic roof with marble tiles. The walls of the circular cella were of porous stone covered with a coloured imitation of bricks. Nine corinthian contact columns decorated the interior, along with a semicircular pedestal for five gold-and-ivory statues of the Macedonian royal family, made by Leohares.

Hereon (4).

The temple of Hera was built around 600 b.C. over an older temple of the 7th century. It was a peripteral construction with wooden columns, 6 × 16, which were gradually replaced by stone columns, this being the reason for their differences in proportion, number of flutings and shapes of capitals. The temple is oblong (50 metres long, 18.75 wide) and low (7.80 metres). The upper parts of the Wall were of brick with a wooden entablature, archaic features that were kept until its final destruction. The interior was divided into three naves by two colonnades. Each second column was linked to the outside wall by a small transversal wall, thus forming 4-5 recesses. At the far end of the cella, standing on pedestals, were the statues of Hera on the throne and Zeus wearing a helmet. In the 2nd century A.D. the temple had been converted into a treasury for the valuables of the sanctuary. To its east we can now see the altar of the temple (8).

Pelopion (5).

This is a hillock of a 31-34 metre diameter, covering a cenotaph of the end of the second millenary b.C., dedicated to funeral offerings in honour of Pelops. It is enclosed in a pentagonal yard with its entrance to the west —a typical characteristic of buildings dedicated to infernal worship. A propylon was added in the 5th century, later reconstructed by the Romans.

Nymphaeon or Exhedra of Herod Atticus (9).

Constructed by Herod Atticus in 160 A.D. in honour of his wife Regilla who had been a priestess of Demeter Chamyne in 155 A.D. A semi-circular reservoir collected the waters of Miraka Aqueduct and through its five spouts (lion-head shaped) chanelled it to a lower oblong reservoir whence through another pipe, reached

13

all parts of the sanctuary. It was a monumental construction faced with marble. At the end of the lower reservoir stood a small circular peristylion with a sacred vase in its middle. The upper semicircular wall had recesses which held statues of the members of Herod's family and the emperor's family.

Treasuries (10, 11, 12).

A series of twelve small chapels, founded during the 5th and 6th centuries b.C. at the foot of the Kronion, they were meant to contain the precious votive offerings of cities, especially the colonies. With the exception of the treasuries of Gela (m) and Metaponte (k) they are all rectangular cellas with a narrow prodomos and two pillars between the antae of the façade. The treasury of Gela (m) had already been erected before the middle of the 6th century facing the east. At the beginning of the 5th century it was altered and a peristyle was added to its southern side. The pediments of the treasuries of Epidamnus (f), Byzantium (g), Cyrene (i) and Megara (l) bore 6th century sculptures figuring the battle of the Giants. It is believed that the small cella west of the treasury of Sicyone (b) is a temple of Eilithya and Sosipolis. Somewhere nearby must have stood the Ideon Andron for the worship of Rea.

The stepped basis (12) supporting the treasuries' terrace was made after 330 b.C. and the supporting wall of the Kronion (10) is also a later construction.

Metroon (13).

At the beginning of the 4th century a doric temple dedicated to the Mother of Gods was built east of the Hereon, consisting of 6 × 11 columns, its dimensions being 20.67 × 10.62 metres with a total height of 7.5 metres. Later the Romans turned it into a temple of Augustus.

Pedestals of the Zannes (14).

The first six Zannes —bronze statues of Zeus— were made in 336 b.C. from the fine paid by the Thessalian boxer Eupolos for bribing his competitors and by the competitors themselves. The second set was covered by the fine paid by the Athenian Callippos in 332 b.C.

Stadium (15, 16, 17).

What is left today of the Stadium are the remains of the classical Stadium III, bearing the additions made by the Romans. The domed entrance (Krypti) was added during the Hellenistic era.

The first monumental Stadium II (16) of the middle 5th century was, like the archaic Stadium I (15) a complement of the Altis. The track reached some 80 metres west and 9 metres south of Stadium II, with slopy banks on the longer embankments only. Stadium III (17) was built around the middle of the 4th century with slopy tiers on all four sides. The track was surrounded by a stone gutter with basins at intervals, curving slightly outwards in the middle of the long sides. The starting and the finishing lines (for «stadion» the starting point was the eastern side, for «diavlos» both the starting and the finishing points were on the western line) still show the two parallel incisions provided to support the toes and the heel of the runners during the start, as well as the holes for the bars marking the tracks for the twenty runners. The total length of the track is 212.75 metres and the distance between the starting point and the finishing line is 192.27 metres = 600 ft = one Olympian stadion. A bit before the finishing line, on the south, stood the tribune of the judges (Hellanodices) with seats placed right behind a low banister of 14 pillars. During the early Roman days (Stadium IV) the Krypti was enlarged by a propylon overlooking the Altis and its south embankment was increased in height. During the 2nd century A.D. (Stadium V) the embankments were reinforced anew and five rows of wooden seats were placed in the northern one for the first time. The altar of Demeter Chamyni standing in the middle of the northern side was built during the same period.

The Echo Portico (18).

This was built after 350 b.C. and its 44 doric columns provided a delicious boundary for the eastern side of the sanctuary, while its back wall served as a supporting wall to the western embankment of the Stadium. It was 96.50 metres long with a width of 12.50

metres, comprising an inner ionian colonnade and a series of storerooms on the side of the Stadium. Its first name was «Poecile» (varied) because of the varied paintings on its walls. But its exceptional accoustics made for its naming into Echo Portico or Eptaphonos in the Roman era.

Southeastern Edifice (20).

South of the Echo Portico the remains of the foundations of a large building were found, with four square rooms in one line and a U-shaped portico facing the Altis (19 pillars on the western and 8 on the southern sides). It may have been the Temple of Hestia or the Prytaneum of the Pisates of the early 5th century. In the beginnings of the 4th century it was surrounded by a portico probably to be used as a room for VIPs. Its largest part was destroyed upon building the House of Nero.

House of Nero, Arch, Octagonon (21, 22, 23).

The House (21) and the triumphal Arch nearby (23) were built in 67 b.C. on the occasion of Nero's visit. Many rooms around the Peristylion and, slightly to the east, a huge octagonal building (22) made of bricks are still to be seen. This latter construction must have been thermal baths.

Temple of Zeus (26).

The temple was built from money raised from the booty taken by the Elians at their war against the rebellious communities of Pisa and Trifylia (472-468 b.C.). After ten years of work the building was completed by 456 b.C. and it was the largest such construction in Greece. Its Elian architect Livon used stone faced with white powdered marble. The roof tiles and the sculptured decorations (vide page 25 etc.), were of Paros marble with later additions of Pendelikon marble.

The temple stands on a large base with steps; the upper one, the «stylobate», was 64.12 × 27.68 metres large. The total height of the building goes beyond 20 metres and was accessible, as most

Peloponesian temples, through a leaning slope at the eastern front. It was a doric peripteral edifice with 6 × 13 columns (height 10.43 metres, bottom diameter 2.21-2.25 metres). The front (prodomos) and the back (opisthodomos) façades, each had two pillars between the doorway sides and friezes with sculptured metopes (page 27).

Inside, the cella had two 7-pillar colonnades with galleries over the side naves, which could be reached by stairways thus enabling the visitors to have a closer look at the gold-and-ivory statue of Zeus. On the level of the second pillar stood a balustrade which isolated the pedestal of the statue (9.67 × 6.65 metres) and the floor before it —made of Elefsis blue stone— to collect the oil with which the statue was annointed to preserve its ivory.

Phidias' statue of Zeus was, together with its pedestal, 12.40 metres high. He was seated on a throne, crowned with olive-leaves, holding in his right hand a statuette of Victory and a sceptre with eagle in his left hand. The face, the torso, the arms and legs were of ivory, while the himation (garment) and the sandals of gold sheets. The ebony and bronze throne was studded with gems. The bronze inside was sculptured with dancing victories, Graces, Hours, Sphinxes, gods, heroes, mythological themes.

The temple must have been altered at least nine times —as is evident from its marble gutters. During the hellenistic era the floor of the front was covered while the Romans later on tiled the slopy entrance of the eastern façade with marble.

Bouleuterion (29).

This constituted the headquarters of the Elian Senate and the Judges; it was also a place for keeping the archives of the Games and for trials of athletes' misdemeanours, for solving differences between them. It consisted of two identical oblong buildings, terminating in an apse on the west and a colonnade inside. The two buildings dated from the 5th and the 6th centuries respectively. The yard in the middle contained the statue of Zeus Horkios. The hellenistic era (3rd or 2nd century b.C.) witnessed the construction of the eastern ionian portico and later the Romans added a doric U-shaped portico.

Transversal cut of the temple of Zeus

South Portico (31).

Built in 365 b.C. it was open on its southern side and had 34
doric columns with a kind of small vestibule shaped by six pillars
in the middle of its southern side. The portico constituted the monumental entrance to the sanctuary. Most probably in the earlier
days very important visitors were received here too. It was 80
metres long with a corinthian colonnade inside.

Leonideon (33).

It served as a hostel built in 330-320 b.C. by Leonidas of Naxos,
measuring 80.18 × 73.52 metres. It had rooms around an inner
atrium with a 44 doric columns peristylion around it. The whole
compound is contained in a colonnade of 138 ionian columns. In

the days of Emperor Hadrian alterations changed the atrium in the fashion of roman villas by adding a large basin with grass plots in it.

Phidias's Workshop (34, 35).

In the spot where later in the 5th century A.D. the early christian basilica (34) was built, stood an ancient building corresponding to the shape and dimensions of the cella of the temple of Zeus (32.18 × 14.50 metres). Phidias had set up in its middle his shaft for the gold-and-ivory statue. The various materials were prepared and worked on in the smaller workrooms (35), ruins of which were found alongside the southern part of the church, and in them the terracotta moulds for the golden parts of the statue, quantities of ivory, bones, volcanic stones, glass, paint, various utensils and an earthenware pot with the inscription FEIDIOEIMI (I belong to Phidias-vide fig. 31 b). These findings trace the erection of the statue of Zeus between 437-420 b.C.

Theokoleon (36).

A mid-4th century building which served as residence for priests, with eight rooms around a central courtyard with columns. In the Roman days an atrium surrounded by a peristylion and more rooms was added on the eastern side.

Roman Hostels (38).

These two buildings stood on the west of Phidias' workshop and were built in the 1st and the 2nd century A.D. What is left of them today are only the foundations from which we can trace a courtyard with a peristylion and several rooms around other courtyards with mosaic floors and wells.

Baths (32, 37, 39, 40, 41, 45).

Ruins to the west of the Theokoleon present a circular foundation within a rectangular hall with a vestibule on its western side (37). This was probably a late-5th century thermal bath which was in the hellenistic and roman eras converted into a heroes' memorial monument. Another compound of greek baths stood on the Northwestern corner of the Palestra (41). A 4th century room with shallow tubs and a similar larger room of late-4th century to the Northwest of the first one can be seen. Slightly to the south there is a roman bath with a «hypocaust» heating system of the year 100 b.C. Between this building and the Kladeos river lay the swimming pool (24 × 16 metres) of the 5th century, which is the only known of its kind in the classical years (40). Iy was destroyed when the Kladeos Thermal Baths were constructed in 100 A.D. This was the largest compound (39) of the three roman baths of the sanctuary; the other two were the so-called South (32) and North (45) thermal baths.

Palestra (42).

A square construction with sides of over 66 metres long, with a central colonnaded courtyard and rooms around it (training areas, baths, dressing rooms, philosophers' and orators' quarters). The outer walls were of brick in their upper parts, the courtyard columns were doric and those of the rooms ionian. The main entrance was on the Northwestern corner. The building is slightly older than the Gymnasium, dating around 200 b.C.

Gymnasium (43, 44).

A rectangular open area over 200 metres long with doric galleries on its four sides for the training of light sports and foot racing. The southern and the double eastern galleries, still seen today, were probably used for training in bad weather. A propylon with two interior colonnades stands on the Northeastern corner.

GUIDE TO THE PLAN OF THE SANCTUARY

1. Prytaneum.
2. Geometric altar of Hestia.
3. Philippeion.
4. Heroon.
5. Pelopion.
6. Houses of the 2nd millenary b.C.
7. Presumed position of the altar of Zeus.
8. Altar of Hereon.
9. Nympheon or Exhedra of Herod Atticus.
10. Kronion supporting wall.
11. Treasuries:

    a) Ilithias Sanctuary.
    b) Sicyon.
    c) Unknown.
    d) Unknown.
    e) Syracuse.
    f) Epidamnos.
    g) Byzantium.
    h) Sybaris.
    i) Cyrene.
    j) Selinus.
    k) Metaponte.
    l) Megara.
    m) Gela.

12. Terrace of Treasuries.
13. Metroon.
14. Pedestals of the Zannes.
15. Locality of Stadium I.
16. Locality of Stadium II.
17. Stadium III-V.
18. Echo Portico.
19. Pedestal of Ptolemee's Offering.
20. Southeastern Edifice.
21. House of Nero.
22. Octagone.
23. Nero's triumphal arch.
24. Pedestal of the statue of victory.
25. Pedestal of Achaean heroes.
26. Temple of Zeus.
27. 4th century b.C. Altis enclosure.
28. Roman enclosure.
29. Bouleterion.
30. Areas connected to the Bouleuterion.
31. South Portico.
32. South thermal baths.
33. Leonideon.
34. Phidias' workshop-early christian basilica.
35. Workshops.
36. Theokoleon.
37. Greek baths-Heroon.
38. Roman hostels.
39. Kladeos thermal baths.
40. Pool.
41. Greek baths.
42. Palestra.
43. Gymnasium.
44. Gymnasium propylon.
45. North thermal baths.

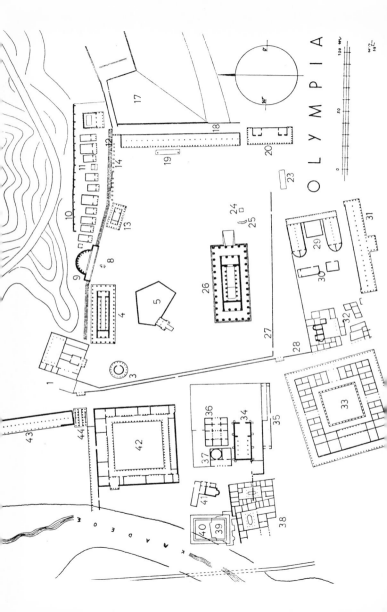

OLYMPIA

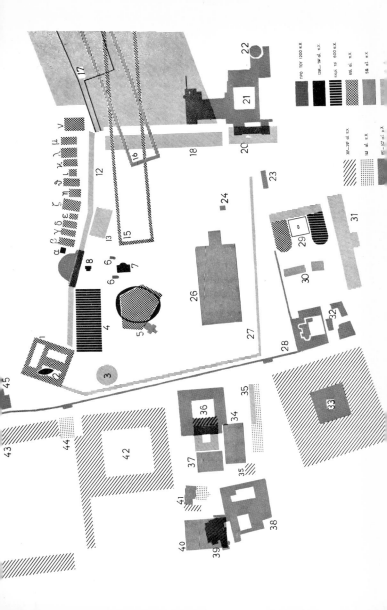

4. The Museum.

Most pieces in the Museum of Olympia are votive offerings i.e. thanksgiving gifts to Zeus for some victory in a war or a contest. The rest are ruins from the architectural decoration of various buildings in the Altis. These were rarely found on the very spots they had originally been placed, because of the changes brought about from time to time in the various parts of the Altis.

There are antiques from the geometric era (9th-8th cent. b.C.) such as numerous bronze and earthenware animal idols, especially bulls and horses (fig. 31) which were usually offered either as independent offerings or, especially the bronze horses, were just handle decorations of tripod cups —prizes of the early Olympic Games. A theme often repeated is a man pulling a horse from its harness or a «synoris» two-horse charriot with its charioteer (fig. 27). These stand together with other rare topics such as hunting scenes with fidgeting animals. Helmeted men's figures with raised hands are believed to be the appearing Zeus. Other statues of warriors, helmeted and with a spear in their raised right arm, are also believed to portray Zeus who offered war victories to the Dorians. In fact Zeus was shown in this position in his first statue standing inside the Hereon. Later, in the archaic and the beginning of the classical eras, the god is presented according to athletic standards and he is shown casting a thunderbolt (fig. 30) until Phidias chose to portray him, in mid-5th century, as a god of peace, master of men and gods (page 17).

The end of the geometric years and the following archaic period (7th-6th century b.C.) are marked with numerous valuable weapon offerings. Helmets of corinthian, illyrian and Halkidiki styles, cuirasses (fig. 15), arm cuirasses (table 16 a), leg cuirasses (fig. 16 b) and shields (fig. 14), most of them richly decorated, were mainly from booty taken after victorious wars, as seen from the inscriptions on them. They were hung on the slopes of the Stadium and as time went by or following some rearrangement of the dike they were fixed in those spots. Some of the best pieces are a Persian helmet, taken by the Athenians during the Persian Wars, and a corinthian one offered to Zeus by Miltiades after his victory at Marathon (fig. 17 b).

Cups are no longer given as prizes but they continued to be

offered in the 7th and the early 6th centuries in their new shape borrowed from eastern art. Busts of griffins (fig. 10) and lions, bull heads (fig. 9 a) and sirene busts (fig. 8) were adorning magnificent cups, many of which had been directly imported from assyrian workshops (fig. 9 a, b).

Bronze sculpture is very developed in mid-5th century as seen from statuettes of gods (fig. 30), heroes (fig. 11) and athletes (fig. 29) which offer an idea of what monumental sculpture looked like in the Altis in those days. The laconian workshops in particular but also the argolian, gave excellent works of art, either with independent works (fig. 23, 30) or with decorations of pots and other utensils (mainly figures from myths, as for instance those in fig. 11 and 12). Forged metal sheets with very elaborate decorations have been found in large numbers, originating mostly from the facing of wooden architectural parts, statues, shields (fig. 14), boxes (fig. 13) and other utensils.

Monumental sculpture on stone is representing archaic laconic art, its best being the head of Hera (fig. 28) of the early 6th century, which is usually related to the worship statue at the Hereon. A late-6th century piece is the basrelief of the Treasury of Megara portraying the Battle of the Giants.

Close to the end of the 6th century and the beginning of the 5th, monumental sculpture on terracotta comes into the scene presenting in Olympia some of its best specimen, compounds of figures which were either adorning buildings we know nothing about (e.g. the Running Victory and the compound of a Selinos and a Maenad), or were independent votive offerings standing in the Altis or inside one of the treasuries. A remarkable piece is a warrior (fig. 18) from a compound executed in a corinthian workshop in 490 b.C. and a representation of the battle of the Giants gives us the head of Athena (fig. 19). Zeus abducting Ganymede and escaping to Mount Olympus (fig. 20) is the masterpiece of this group, a work of 470 b.C. with brilliant colours and expressive faces with a scale of expressions of age, character and feelings (vide cover illustration).

Several pieces from the tiling and the terracotta facing of the wooden parts of the roofs of buildings in the Altis were kept, with a large variety of decorative themes, remarkable designs and bright colours (fig. 21, 22).

The decade from 565-555 b.C., following the Persian Wars, offers us the magnificent compound of the sculptures from the temple of Zeus, a landmark in the history of Greek art.

Most of the fragments from figures of the pediments were found during the german excavations (1875-1880) where they had fallen as a result of earthquakes in the 6th century b.C., or in walls of houses where they had been used as building material by the early christian settlers in the Altis.

The eastern pediment represented the most important local legend, the charriot contest between Oenomaos and Pelops. Oenomaos, king of Pisa, had been given the oracle that he would lose both his kingdom and his life by the husband of his daughter Hippodamia. He therefore decided to give her hand to whomever would beat him in a charriot race. Oenomaos competed with 13 suitors whom he beat and executed, until the arrival of Pelops, who, thanks to Hippodamia, convinced Myrtilos —Oenomaos' charioteer— to remove one of the nails holding Oenomaos' charriot wheels to the vehicle; consequently, during the competition, the wheel went off the charriot and Oenomaos got killed.

The eastern pediment represents the preparation for this contest. In the middle, unseen yet present, stands Zeus (fig. 34), with bearded Oenomaos and young Pelops on his left and right, each having his mate by his side, Steropi and Hippodamia. Kneeling before the quadrigas are a maid and a young server (fig. 35, 36). Behind the left charriot stands Myrtilos and behind the right one the old foreteller sadly foresees the outcome of the competition (fig. 27). A second foreteller is to be seen on the left side and the composition ends with personifications of Alfios on the left and Kladios rivers on the right (fig. 38). The tragic fate of the house of Oenomaos floats over all the figures in the pediment still, meditative and lonely as they stand.

The western pediment represents the combat of the Centaurs, from the legend where during the wedding of the King of the Lapithae Pirithoos, the Centaurs became drunk and assaulted the wives and children of the Lapithae.

In the midst of the wild fight stands Appollo, serene and majestic (fig. 39), watching over order. Two Centaurs, on his left right, have caught a Lapithan woman each (fig. 40) and are attacked by Theseus and Pirithoos. On their sides Centaurs and Lapithans fighting

26

(fig. 41) and next to them compositions of three persons symmetrically placed on their sides, a Lapithan woman, the Centaur catching her and the Lapithan rescuing her. The end corners are occupied by two reclining Lapithan women watching the fight; the two elderly women and the young girl of the left corner are works of a later period, probably replacing the original which may have been destroyed during an earthquake.

The artist who designed and made the decorations of the pediments are not known. This, and the reconstitution of the pediments to their original shape are problems faced by archaeologists since last century, without, however, having reached any final conclusion (fig. 33 presents two of the most probable solutions).

The metopes of the entrance and the rear porch friezes were adorned with works representing the Labours of Hercules, a panhellenic hero and son of Zeus and an ideal standard for the sporting youth in Olympia. For the first time the full line of dodecathlon (the 12 labours) is presented as a whole, starting with the lion of Nemea, followed by the Hydra of Lerna, Hercules offering to Athena the Birds of Stymphalia, the Cretan Bull, the horned deer, Hercules capturing the Amazon Hippolyta's girdle. On the eastern side, from left to right, appalled Eurystheus at the sight of the Arcadian boar, Diomedes' horses, Hercules fighting Geryon the triple-bodied monster, Atlas and the apples of the Hesperides, Hercules and Cerberus, and, in an outstanding position on the northeastern corner, the main Elian legend; Hercules cleansing the Augean Stables (vide scetch on page 27 and fig. 45-49). Many of the pediment pieces are now in the Louvre, taken by members of the Expedition Scientifique de Morèe right after the first excavations in Olympia in 1829.

One of the best original sculptures of the classical era, which has been preserved until today, is the statue of Victory (fig. 50-52). It was standing on a 9-metre triangular pedestal before the Northeastern corner of the temple of Zeus. From the inscriptions on its base it appears to have been a votive offering of the Messinians and the Naupactians from the booty taken from the Sfacterians in 425 b.C. It was a work of Paeonios of Mende in Chalkidice, who had also executed the eastern «acroteria» of the temple (Alkamenis had made the left ones).

Victory's himation, as blown by a breeze, floats and carries

27

her to the skies. The thin veil is pushed backwards and uncovers an almost bare body. With stretched wings and a palm leaf in her right hand, it looks as though she is barely touching the cloud out of which emerges Zeus' other herald, the eagle. This is the first truly flighing figure in greek art, unique in the technique of its equilibrium (note the forward motion of the axis of the face and the uniform massive marble piece of the himation). And the aesthetic outcome of all these is admirable; the figure is practically floating in all its beauty.

The most renowned of the exhibits in the Museum of Olympia is Hermes (fig. 23, 24, 53), considered an original work by Praxiteles. The problem of its genuineness has not yet found its solution. Nevertheless the majority think it is a work of Praxiteles of the year 330 b.C., which the Romans «modernised», mainly by polishing it.

Hermes is presented carrying baby Dionysos to Nissa, to be raised by the Nymphs after his mother Semeli died. He stops to rest a while leaning with his left elbow on a tree trunk, which he covered with his himation and is trying to entertain the child with a bunch of grapes he holds in his right hand. The statue bears all the characteristics of Praxiteles' art, the elasticity of the young body, the lovely curve of his body as it rests its weight on one leg, and the trunk, the sweetness of the face with the dreamy look.

The statue was found in the Hereon in 1877 and was probably a votive offering to commemorate the peace treaty between the Elians and the Arcadians.

The short revival of the sanctuary during the early imperial days left us a series of statues of roman emperors and other officials, made most by Elians either as tokens of gratitude or flattery. From the temple of Augustus —the ancient Metroon— comes the colossal torso of the statue of Augustus which had been made like that of Zeus, the statues of Emperors Claudius and Titus, and Agrippina the Younger. The beheaded statues of Herod Atticus' family (offerings of the Elians), of Hadrian (fig. 54) from the imperial family, Pius Antoninus and his wife Faustina the Older, Faustina the Younger and her children, etc. were standing on the recesses of the Nympheon, all mediocre pieces of art. Among them was also found the marble bull (fig. 56) from the partition of the reservoirs of the Nympheon bearing the inscription «Regilla priestess of Demeter is the water and what surrounds the water belongs to Zeus».

GENERAL BIBLIOGRAPHY

The monuments of Olympia and the various pieces which were found during the first german excavations were published in five volumes of text and four volumes of tables under the general title OLYMPIA by E. Curtius and F. Adler (1890-1897 edition). The findings of the more recent excavations, from 1937 onwards, have been published in eight volumes entitled «Berichte über die Ausgrabungen in Olympia». The six volumes of «Olympische Forschungen» contain a more detailed presentation of the material found during the excavations till nowadays.

ILLUSTRATIONS

1. Northeastern corner of Hereon.
2. Overall view of Hereon.
3. Bases of the Zannes and entrance to the Stadium (Krypte).
4. General view of the Stadium.
5. Temple of Zeus.
6. Philippeion.
7. Palestra.
8. Bronze bust of a sirene from the decoration of a cup (700-670 b.C.).
9. a) Bronze bust of a bull, from the decoration of a cup; imported work of art from the east; end of 8th cent. b.C.
   b) Bronze bust of a male sirene; imported work of art from the east; end of 8th cent. b.C.
10. Bronze bust of a griffin from the decoration of a cup; latter part of the 7th century.
11. a) Bronze statuette of a warrior from a vase decoration of 550 b.C.
    b) Similar statuette of an old man from the same vessel.
12. a) A pair of sphinxes from a bronze vessel; 1st half of the 6th century.
    b) Bronze statue of silinos; 2nd half of the 6th century.
13. Bronze sheets portraying Kaeneos between two Centaurs; 650 b.C.
14. Bronze shield insignia with a mermaid-like monster. End of 6th century.
15. Bronze cuirass; latter part of the 6th century.

16. a) Bronze arm cuirass. 2nd half of the 6th century.
    b) Bronze leg cuirass. 2nd half of the 6th century.
17. a) Bronze corinthian helmet decorated with silver and ivory; 2nd half of the 7th century.
    b) Bronze corinthian helmet; offering by Miltiades; later than 490 b.C.
18. Terracotta trunk of a warrior; about 490 b.C.
19. Terracotta head of Athina; about 490 b.C.
20. Terracotta compound portraying the abduction of Ganymede by Zeus; about 470 b.C.
21. a) Terracotta acroterion of an unknown treasury; 2nd half of the 6th century.
    b) Terracotta decoration of an unknown treasury; 2nd half of the 6th century.
22. a) Corner acroceramus from Phidias' workshop; about 430 b.C.
    b) Terracotta decoration from Phidias' workshop; about 430 b.C.
23. Statue of Hermes; by Praxiteles; about 330 b.C.
24. Head of the statue of Hermes.
25. Reconstruction of the temple of Zeus.
26. Bronze statuette of a warrior (Zeus); early 7th century.
27. Bronze statuette of the charioteer of a synoris; 2nd half of the 8th century.
28. Huge head of Hera's statue; early 6th century.
29. Bronze statue of a runner. On his right thigh the inscription TODIFOSIMI, 480-470 b.C.
30. Bronze statuette of Zeus casting a thunderbolt; 470-460 b.C.
31. a) Bronze statuette of a horse; 8th century b.C.
    b) Base of a terracotta wine-tumbler (with a probable autograph by Phidias); 430 b.C.
32. Statuette of a horse from a bronze quadriga; 470 b.C.
33. a) Reconstruction of the eastern pediment of the temple of Zeus; as per Studniczka.
    b) Reconstruction of the western pediment of the temple of Zeus, as per Tren.
34. Zeus, from the eastern pediment.
35. Zeus, Pelops, Hippodamia (?) and the young server; eastern pediment.

31

36. Oenomaos, Steropi (?), the maid and the right side quadriga.
37. The right side foreteller; eastern pediment.
38. Kladeos; eastern pediment.
39. Apollo; western pediment.
40. The central figures of the western pediment.
41. Diiamea and Centaur Eurition; western pediment.
42. The Lapithan woman of the right side compound; western pediment.
43. The Lapithan women of the left side compound; western pediment.
44. Centaur and a Lapithan.
45. The metope of the Birds of Stymphalia.
46. The metope of the Cretan Bull.
47. The metope of Atlas.
48. The metope of the Cerberus.
49. The metope of the Augean Stables.
50. Statue of Victory; by Paenios; 425-420 b.C.
51. Statue of Victory; by Paeonios; 425-420 b.C.
52. Reconstruction of the statue of Victory.
53. Statue of Hermes; by Praxiteles.
54. Statue of Emperor Hadrian.
55. Bust of Emperor Hadrian's favourite youth Antinoos.
56. Bronze bull from the Exhedra of Herod Atticus; 160 A.D.

Marble

3

8

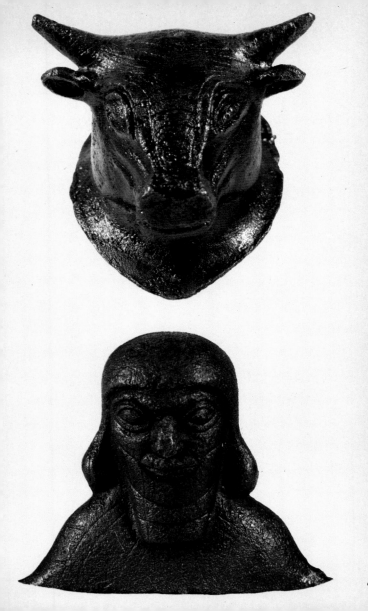

9

10

1

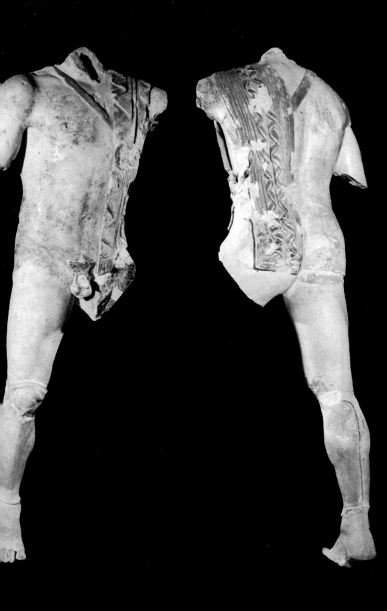

27

ΦΕΙΔ...ΟΕΙ
ΜΙ...

3

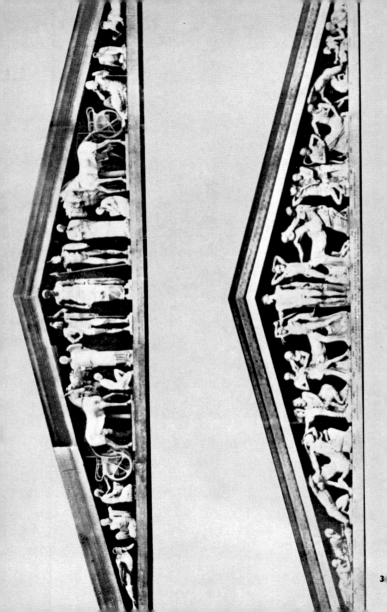

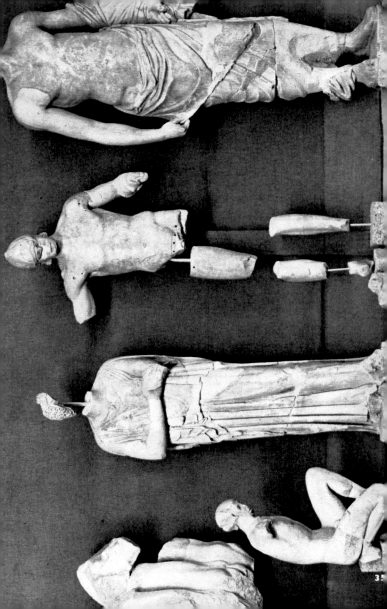

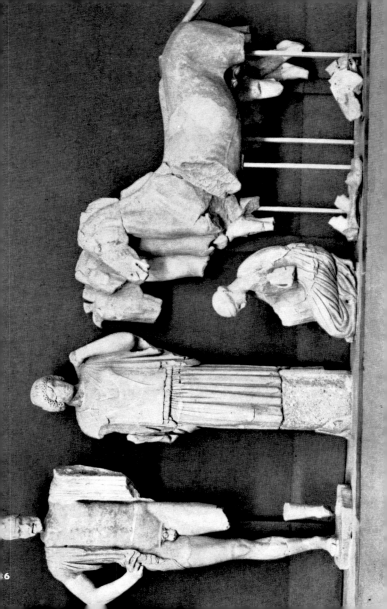

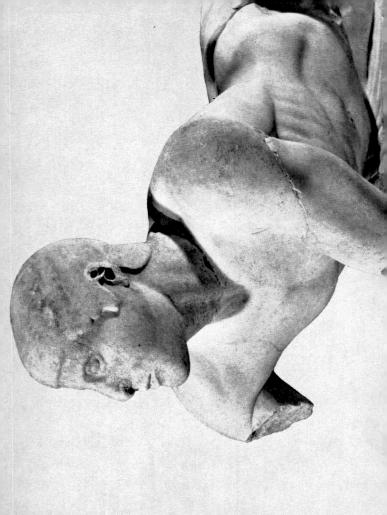

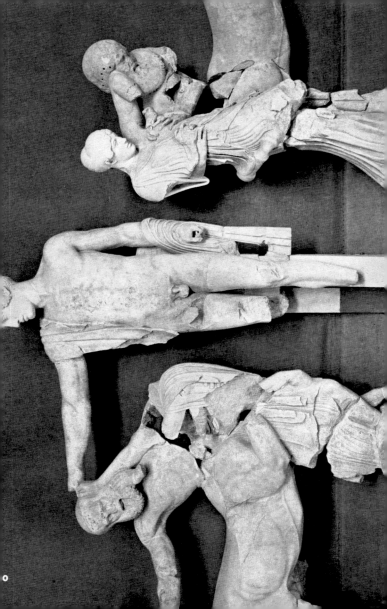

43

45

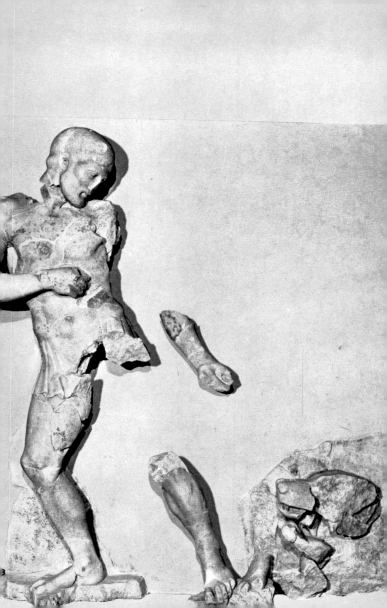